Table Of Contents

- What is SEO? 2
- Importance of SEO in Digital Marketing 2
- Evolution of SEO 2
- Chapter 2: Getting Started with SEO 2
  - Setting SEO Goals 2
  - Understanding Keywords 2
  - Competitor Analysis 2
- Chapter 3: On-Page SEO Best Practices 2
  - Title tags and Meta descriptions 2
  - Image optimization 2
  - URL structure 2
- Chapter 4: Off-Page SEO Tactics 2
  - Link building strategies 2
  - Social media optimization 2
  - Guest blogging 2
- Chapter 5: E-commerce SEO Strategies 2
  - Product page optimization 2
  - Category page optimization 2
  - Mobile optimization for e-commerce sites 2
- Chapter 6: Technical SEO Audit and Analysis 2
  - Website speed optimization 2
  - Mobile responsiveness 2
  - Structured data markup 2
- Chapter 7: Top Google Ranking Techniques 2
  - Google algorithm updates 2
  - Local SEO strategies 2
  - Featured snippets and rich snippets 2
- Chapter 8: Advanced SEO Strategies For Google, Yahoo and Bing 2
  - Secret SEO Tools 2
  - Yahoo SEO Tips 2
  - Google SEO Tips 2
  - Bing SEO Tips 2

- Chapter 9: Monitoring and Measuring SEO Success 2
  - Google Analytics and Search Console 2
  - Key performance indicators for SEO 2
  - Reporting and analysis 2
- Chapter 10: Conclusion and Next Steps 2
  - Recap of SEO strategies 2
  - Continuing education and staying updated 2
  - Taking your SEO skills to the next level 2
- Chapter 1: Introduction to SEO 1

Chapter 1: Introduction to SEO

What is SEO?

What is SEO? Search Engine Optimization (SEO) is the practice of optimizing your website to improve its visibility and ranking on search engines like Google. In simple terms, SEO helps your website appear higher in search results when users search for relevant keywords or phrases. This is crucial for businesses looking to attract more organic traffic to their website and increase their online presence.

SEO involves a combination of strategies and techniques aimed at improving various aspects of your website, such as content, keywords, meta tags, and backlinks. By optimizing these elements, you can increase your chances of ranking higher on search engine results pages (SERPs) and driving more organic traffic to your site.

One of the key benefits of SEO is that it can help you attract highly targeted traffic to your website. By targeting specific keywords and phrases that are relevant to your business, you can attract users who are actively searching for products or services like yours. This can result in higher conversion rates and increased sales for your business.

In addition to improving your website's visibility and driving more organic traffic, SEO can also help you build credibility and authority in your niche. When your website ranks highly in search results, users are more likely to trust your brand and view you as an industry leader. This can help you attract more customers and establish a strong online presence.

Overall, SEO is a powerful digital marketing strategy that can help businesses of all sizes improve their online visibility, attract more organic traffic, and increase their revenue. By implementing effective SEO tactics and staying up-to-date with the latest trends and algorithms, you can achieve top Google rankings and drive success for your business in the competitive online landscape.

Importance of SEO in Digital Marketing

SEO, or search engine optimization, plays a crucial role in the success of any digital marketing strategy. In today's competitive online landscape, it is essential for businesses to implement effective SEO tactics in order to improve their visibility and attract more organic traffic to their websites. By optimizing their websites for search engines, businesses can increase their chances of ranking higher in search engine results pages, ultimately driving more targeted traffic to their site.

One of the key benefits of SEO in digital marketing is its ability to improve a website's visibility in search engine results pages. By optimizing your website for relevant keywords and phrases, you can increase your chances of ranking higher in search engine results pages, making it easier for potential customers to find your website when searching for products or services related to your business. This increased visibility can lead to higher levels of organic traffic, as well as increased brand awareness and recognition.

In addition to improving visibility, SEO can also help businesses attract more targeted traffic to their websites. By targeting specific keywords and phrases that are relevant to your business, you can attract visitors who are actively searching for products or services that you offer. This targeted traffic is more likely to convert into leads or sales, as these visitors are already interested in what you have to offer. By optimizing your website for search engines, you can attract more of these high-quality leads, ultimately increasing your chances of success in the digital marketplace.

Furthermore, SEO can help businesses improve their overall online presence and credibility. By ranking higher in search engine results pages, businesses can establish themselves as authorities in their industry, gaining the trust and confidence of potential customers. This increased credibility can help businesses attract more leads and sales, as customers are more likely to choose a business that appears at the top of search engine results pages. By implementing effective SEO tactics, businesses can build a strong online presence that sets them apart from their competitors.

Overall, the importance of SEO in digital marketing cannot be overstated. By optimizing your website for search engines, you can improve your visibility, attract more targeted traffic, and establish yourself as a credible authority in your industry. Whether you are a small business looking to increase your online visibility or a large corporation seeking to dominate the search engine rankings, implementing effective SEO tactics is essential for success in the digital marketplace.

Evolution of SEO

In the ever-evolving world of digital marketing, the evolution of SEO (Search Engine Optimization) has been a crucial factor in determining the success of online businesses. From its humble beginnings to its current state as a powerful tool for improving website visibility and rankings on search engines, SEO has come a long way.

At its inception, SEO was primarily focused on keyword optimization and link building. Websites would stuff keywords into their content in an attempt to manipulate search engine algorithms and improve their rankings. However, as search engines became more sophisticated, these tactics became less effective and even harmful to a website's reputation.

As search engines like Google began to prioritize user experience and quality content, SEO strategies had to adapt to keep up with the changing landscape. This shift led to the development of on-page SEO best practices, which focus on optimizing individual web pages to improve their search engine rankings. This includes optimizing meta tags, headings, and content for relevant keywords, as well as improving site speed and mobile-friendliness.

Off-page SEO tactics also became increasingly important as search engines began to value high-quality backlinks from reputable websites. This led to the rise of link-building strategies, such as guest posting, influencer outreach, and social media marketing, to improve a website's authority and credibility in the eyes of search engines.

Today, SEO has become a multifaceted discipline that encompasses a wide range of strategies and techniques to improve a website's visibility and rankings on search engines. From technical SEO audit and analysis to E-commerce SEO strategies, businesses must stay up-to-date with the latest trends and best practices to succeed in the competitive online landscape. As the digital marketing industry continues to evolve, so too must SEO, in order to drive organic traffic and achieve top Google rankings for businesses of all sizes and industries.

Chapter 2: Getting Started with SEO

Setting SEO Goals

Setting SEO goals is a crucial step in any successful SEO strategy. Without clearly defined goals, it can be difficult to measure the success of your efforts and make adjustments as needed. When setting SEO goals, it is important to consider what you hope to achieve with your SEO efforts. Are you looking to increase your website's visibility on search engines? Improve your website's ranking for specific keywords? Drive more organic traffic to your site? By clearly defining your goals, you can create a roadmap for your SEO strategy and measure your progress along the way.

One common goal for many businesses is to improve their website's ranking on Google. Achieving a top Google ranking can significantly increase your website's visibility and drive more organic traffic to your site. To set this goal, you may want to focus on optimizing your website for relevant keywords, improving your website's loading speed, creating high-quality content, and building quality backlinks. By setting specific, measurable goals for each of these areas, you can track your progress and make adjustments as needed to improve your website's ranking on Google.

Another important goal for many businesses is to improve their e-commerce SEO strategies. E-commerce websites face unique challenges when it comes to SEO, such as managing large product catalogs, optimizing product pages, and implementing structured data markup. By setting goals to improve your e-commerce SEO strategies, you can focus on key areas such as optimizing product descriptions, improving site navigation, and implementing schema markup to enhance your website's visibility on search engines.

In addition to setting goals for on-page SEO best practices, it is also important to set goals for off-page SEO tactics. Off-page SEO tactics, such as building quality backlinks, social media marketing, and influencer partnerships, can help improve your website's authority and credibility in the eyes of search engines. By setting goals to increase the number of quality backlinks to your site, improve your social media engagement, and build relationships with influencers in your industry, you can enhance your website's off-page SEO efforts and drive more organic traffic to your site.

In conclusion, setting SEO goals is essential for any successful SEO strategy. By clearly defining your goals, such as improving your website's ranking on Google, enhancing your e-commerce SEO strategies, and implementing on-page and off-page SEO tactics, you can create a roadmap for your SEO efforts and measure your progress along the way. By setting specific, measurable goals for each area of your SEO strategy, you can track your progress and make adjustments as needed to achieve SEO success and drive more organic traffic to your site.

Understanding Keywords

In the world of search engine optimization (SEO), understanding keywords is crucial to achieving success in improving your website's visibility on search engines like Google. Keywords are the words or phrases that users type into search engines to find information, products, or services. By optimizing your website with relevant keywords, you can increase your chances of ranking higher in search engine results pages (SERPs) and driving more organic traffic to your site.

Keywords can be categorized into two main types: short-tail keywords and long-tail keywords. Short-tail keywords are broad and general terms that have a high search volume but also high competition. Long-tail keywords, on the other hand, are more specific phrases that have lower search volume but also lower competition. It's important to strike a balance between using both types of keywords in your SEO strategy to attract a diverse range of users to your website.

Keyword research is the foundation of any successful SEO campaign. By conducting thorough keyword research, you can identify the most relevant and high-performing keywords for your website's content. There are various tools available, such as Google Keyword Planner, SEMrush, and Ahrefs, that can help you identify the most relevant keywords for your niche and target audience. It's essential to regularly update and refine your list of keywords based on changes in search trends and user behavior.

Once you have identified your target keywords, it's time to strategically incorporate them into your website's content. This process, known as on-page SEO, involves optimizing your website's meta titles, meta descriptions, headers, and body content with your target keywords. It's important to ensure that your keywords are used naturally and don't disrupt the flow of your content. Additionally, using keywords in your image alt text, URL structure, and internal linking can further improve your website's SEO performance.

In addition to on-page SEO, off-page SEO tactics such as link building and social media marketing can also help boost your website's search engine rankings. By building high-quality backlinks from authoritative websites and engaging with your audience on social media platforms, you can increase your website's credibility and authority in the eyes of search engines. Overall, understanding keywords and how to effectively optimize them is essential for achieving top Google rankings and driving organic traffic to your website.

Competitor Analysis

Competitor analysis is a crucial aspect of any SEO strategy. By understanding the strengths and weaknesses of your competitors, you can better position yourself in the market and gain a competitive edge. In this subchapter, we will explore the importance of competitor analysis in the world of SEO and how you can leverage this information to improve your own rankings.

One of the key benefits of competitor analysis is gaining insight into the strategies that are working for your competitors. By analyzing their content, keywords, and backlink profiles, you can identify opportunities to improve your own SEO efforts. Additionally, studying your competitors can help you identify gaps in the market that you can capitalize on. For example, if you notice that a competitor is ranking well for a certain keyword, you can create content that targets that keyword to compete for the same traffic.

Competitor analysis can also help you identify areas where your competitors are falling short. By analyzing their website structure, user experience, and overall SEO efforts, you can pinpoint areas where you can outperform them. For example, if you notice that a competitor has a slow-loading website or poor-quality content, you can focus on improving these aspects of your own site to attract more visitors.

In addition to studying your direct competitors, it is also important to analyze the broader market landscape. By monitoring industry trends and changes in search engine algorithms, you can stay ahead of the curve and adjust your SEO strategy accordingly. This can help you anticipate changes in the market and position yourself as a leader in your niche.

Overall, competitor analysis is a valuable tool for any SEO professional looking to improve their rankings and drive more traffic to their website. By studying your competitors and the broader market landscape, you can gain valuable insights that will help you stay ahead of the competition and achieve SEO success.

Chapter 3: On-Page SEO Best Practices

Title tags and Meta descriptions

Title tags and meta descriptions are two crucial elements in optimizing your website for search engines. These elements play a significant role in improving your website's visibility and click-through rates on search engine results pages. In this subchapter, we will delve into the importance of title tags and meta descriptions and how you can create them effectively to boost your website's performance.

Title tags are HTML elements that define the title of a webpage. They appear as the clickable headline in search engine results pages and are crucial for conveying the content of your page to both search engines and users. A well-crafted title tag should be concise, descriptive, and relevant to the content on the page. Including targeted keywords in your title tags can also help improve your website's visibility in search results.

Meta descriptions, on the other hand, are brief summaries of a webpage's content that appear below the title tag in search engine results pages. While meta descriptions do not directly impact search engine rankings, they can influence click-through rates by providing users with a preview of the page's content. Writing compelling meta descriptions that accurately summarize the content of your page can entice users to click on your link, increasing traffic to your website.

When creating title tags and meta descriptions, it is essential to keep in mind your target audience and the keywords they are likely to use in their search queries. Conducting keyword research can help you identify the terms and phrases that are most relevant to your content and incorporate them strategically into your title tags and meta descriptions. Additionally, testing different variations of your title tags and meta descriptions can help you determine which ones are most effective in driving traffic to your website.

In conclusion, title tags and meta descriptions are critical components of your SEO strategy that can significantly impact your website's performance in search engine results pages. By optimizing these elements with relevant keywords and compelling content, you can improve your website's visibility, click-through rates, and ultimately, your search engine rankings. Stay tuned for the next section, where we will discuss advanced techniques for optimizing your website's on-page and off-page SEO.

Image optimization

Image optimization is a crucial aspect of SEO that is often overlooked by many website owners. In order to improve your search engine rankings and drive more organic traffic to your site, it is important to optimize the images on your website. By following a few simple tips and best practices, you can ensure that your images are not only visually appealing but also optimized for search engines.

One of the first steps in image optimization is choosing the right file format. JPEG and PNG are the most commonly used file formats for web images, with each having its own advantages and disadvantages. JPEG is best for photographs and images with lots of colors, while PNG is better for images with transparency or text. By choosing the right file format, you can reduce the file size of your images and improve your website's loading speed.

Another important aspect of image optimization is the use of descriptive filenames and alt text. When naming your image files, it is important to use relevant keywords that describe the content of the image. This not only helps search engines understand what the image is about but also improves the overall relevance of your website. Alt text, or alternative text, is a brief description of an image that appears when the image fails to load. By including descriptive alt text for all your images, you can improve accessibility for visually impaired users and enhance your website's SEO.

In addition to descriptive filenames and alt text, it is important to optimize the size and resolution of your images. Large, high-resolution images can slow down your website's loading speed and negatively impact user experience. By resizing and compressing your images, you can improve your website's performance and ensure that your images load quickly on all devices. There are various tools and plugins available that can help you optimize your images without sacrificing quality.

Lastly, it is important to consider the placement and context of your images on your website. Images that are relevant to the surrounding content and enhance the user experience are more likely to be shared and linked to by other websites. By strategically placing images throughout your website and incorporating them into your overall SEO strategy, you can increase your website's visibility and drive more organic traffic. Image optimization is an essential aspect of SEO that should not be overlooked, as it can have a significant impact on your website's search engine rankings and overall success.

URL structure

In the world of SEO, one of the most important factors to consider when optimizing your website is the URL structure. A well-structured URL can not only improve the user experience but also help search engines understand the content of your page better. In this subchapter, we will discuss the importance of URL structure and provide some best practices for creating SEO-friendly URLs.

First and foremost, it is essential to keep your URLs simple and descriptive. Avoid using long strings of numbers or random characters in your URLs, as they can be difficult for users and search engines to understand. Instead, use keywords that accurately describe the content of the page. For example, instead of www.example.com/page1234, use www.example.com/seo-best-practices.

Additionally, it is important to use hyphens to separate words in your URLs. Hyphens are seen as word separators by search engines, while underscores are not. This means that www.example.com/seo-best-practices is more SEO-friendly than www.example.com/seo_best_practices. By using hyphens, you can improve the readability and searchability of your URLs.

Another best practice for URL structure is to keep them as short as possible. Shorter URLs are easier to remember and share, and they also tend to perform better in search engine rankings. Aim to keep your URLs under 50-60 characters to ensure they are displayed properly in search results and are not cut off.

Furthermore, it is important to include relevant keywords in your URLs. Keywords help search engines understand the topic of your page and can improve your chances of ranking for those terms. However, be sure to use keywords naturally and avoid keyword stuffing in your URLs. Instead, focus on creating URLs that accurately reflect the content of the page.

Overall, a well-structured URL can have a significant impact on your SEO efforts. By following these best practices and creating SEO-friendly URLs, you can improve your website's visibility in search engine results and drive more organic traffic to your site. Remember to keep your URLs simple, descriptive, and keyword-rich to maximize your SEO success.

Chapter 4: Off-Page SEO Tactics

Link building strategies

Link building is a crucial aspect of any successful SEO strategy. In this subchapter, we will explore some effective link building strategies that can help boost your website's search engine rankings and increase organic traffic. Link building involves getting other websites to link back to your site, which signals to search engines that your content is valuable and trustworthy.

One of the most important link building strategies is creating high-quality content that naturally attracts backlinks. By creating informative, engaging, and shareable content, you increase the chances of other websites linking back to your site. This can be achieved through blog posts, infographics, videos, and other forms of content that provide value to your target audience.

Another effective link building strategy is reaching out to other websites in your industry and asking them to link back to your site. This can be done through email outreach, social media engagement, or networking at industry events. When reaching out to other websites, be sure to emphasize the value that your content can provide to their audience and why linking to your site would benefit both parties.

Guest blogging is another popular link building strategy that involves writing articles for other websites in your industry in exchange for a backlink to your site. By guest blogging on reputable sites with high domain authority, you can not only increase your website's visibility but also establish yourself as an authority in your niche. Be sure to write high-quality, informative articles that provide value to the readers of the host site.

Lastly, monitoring your backlink profile is essential for effective link building. By regularly analyzing your backlinks and identifying any low-quality or toxic links, you can disavow them to avoid penalties from search engines. Additionally, keeping track of your competitors' backlink profiles can help you identify new link building opportunities and stay ahead in the rankings. By implementing these link building strategies, you can improve your website's search engine rankings and drive more organic traffic to your site.

Social media optimization

Social media optimization is a crucial aspect of any successful SEO strategy. With the rise of social media platforms such as Facebook, Twitter, and Instagram, businesses have a unique opportunity to reach their target audience and drive traffic to their website. By optimizing your social media profiles and sharing engaging content, you can increase your visibility online and improve your search engine rankings.

One of the key components of social media optimization is ensuring that your profiles are fully optimized with relevant keywords and information about your business. This includes using keywords in your profile bio, description, and posts to make it easier for users to find your content when searching for related topics. Additionally, make sure to include a link to your website in your profile so that users can easily navigate to your site.

In addition to optimizing your profiles, it's important to regularly share high-quality content that is relevant to your target audience. This could include blog posts, videos, infographics, and other types of content that will engage your followers and encourage them to visit your website. By consistently posting valuable content, you can build a loyal following and increase your chances of driving traffic to your site.

Another important aspect of social media optimization is engaging with your followers and building relationships with them. This includes responding to comments, messages, and mentions, as well as participating in conversations related to your industry. By actively engaging with your audience, you can create a sense of community around your brand and encourage users to share your content with their own networks.

Overall, social media optimization is an essential component of any comprehensive SEO strategy. By optimizing your profiles, sharing engaging content, and engaging with your followers, you can increase your online visibility, drive traffic to your website, and improve your search engine rankings. By incorporating social media optimization into your overall SEO strategy, you can set yourself up for success in the competitive online landscape.

Guest blogging

Guest blogging is a powerful strategy that can help improve your website's search engine rankings and increase your online visibility. By writing high-quality, relevant content for other websites in your niche, you can attract new audiences and build valuable backlinks to your site. This can help boost your website's authority and improve its chances of ranking higher in search engine results pages.

When it comes to guest blogging, it's important to choose websites that are reputable and have a strong online presence. Look for websites that are relevant to your niche and have a high domain authority. By publishing content on these websites, you can reach a wider audience and establish yourself as an authority in your industry.

When writing guest blog posts, make sure to focus on providing value to the readers. Write informative, engaging content that addresses their needs and interests. Avoid overly promotional content, as this can turn off readers and hurt your chances of being published on other websites. Instead, aim to educate and entertain your audience with valuable insights and actionable tips.

In addition to writing guest blog posts, consider inviting other bloggers to write for your own website. This can help diversify your content and attract new audiences to your site. By collaborating with other bloggers, you can also build valuable relationships in your industry and increase your online visibility.

Overall, guest blogging is a valuable strategy for improving your website's search engine rankings and increasing your online visibility. By writing high-quality, relevant content for other websites in your niche, you can attract new audiences, build valuable backlinks, and establish yourself as an authority in your industry. So, consider incorporating guest blogging into your SEO strategy to take your online presence to the next level.

Chapter 5: E-commerce SEO Strategies

Product page optimization

Product page optimization is a crucial aspect of any successful SEO strategy, especially for e-commerce websites looking to improve their Google rankings and increase organic traffic. By optimizing the product pages on your website, you can improve visibility, drive more targeted traffic, and ultimately increase sales.

One of the key elements of product page optimization is ensuring that each page is unique and optimized for specific keywords related to the product. This includes creating unique title tags, meta descriptions, and product descriptions that include relevant keywords. By incorporating these keywords throughout the page, you can improve your chances of ranking higher in search engine results pages (SERPs).

In addition to keyword optimization, it's also important to optimize the images and videos on your product pages. This includes using descriptive file names, alt text, and captions that include relevant keywords. By optimizing your multimedia content, you can improve the overall user experience and make it easier for search engines to crawl and index your product pages.

Another important aspect of product page optimization is ensuring that your pages load quickly and are mobile-friendly. Slow-loading pages and poor mobile experiences can negatively impact your search engine rankings and user engagement. By optimizing your product pages for speed and mobile responsiveness, you can improve the overall user experience and increase the likelihood of converting visitors into customers.

Overall, product page optimization is a critical component of any successful SEO strategy, especially for e-commerce websites looking to improve their

Google rankings and increase organic traffic. By optimizing your product pages for specific keywords, multimedia content, page speed, and mobile-friendliness, you can improve visibility, drive more targeted traffic, and ultimately increase sales.

Category page optimization

Category page optimization is a critical aspect of SEO that is often overlooked by many e-commerce websites. By optimizing your category pages, you can improve your website's visibility in search engine results and increase your chances of ranking higher on Google. In this chapter, we will explore the best practices for optimizing category pages to drive more organic traffic to your website and ultimately increase your online sales.

One of the first steps in category page optimization is to ensure that each category page is properly optimized for relevant keywords. Conduct keyword research to identify the most relevant and high-volume keywords for each category and incorporate them strategically throughout the page. This will help search engines understand the content of your category pages and rank them higher for relevant search queries.

In addition to keyword optimization, it is important to optimize the meta tags of your category pages. This includes the meta title, meta description, and meta keywords. By optimizing these meta tags with relevant keywords and persuasive language, you can improve click-through rates from search engine results and drive more traffic to your category pages.

Another important aspect of category page optimization is to ensure that your category pages are user-friendly and easy to navigate. Make sure that your category pages have a clear and logical hierarchy, with relevant subcategories and products listed in a structured manner. This will not only improve the user experience but also help search engines crawl and index your category pages more effectively.

Finally, don't forget to optimize your category pages for mobile devices. With the increasing use of smartphones and tablets, it is crucial to ensure that your category pages are responsive and mobile-friendly. By optimizing your category pages for mobile, you can provide a seamless user experience across all devices and improve your chances of ranking higher in mobile search results. By following these best practices for category page optimization, you can improve your website's visibility in search engine results, attract more organic traffic, and ultimately increase your online sales.

Mobile optimization for e-commerce sites

Mobile optimization for e-commerce sites is essential in today's digital landscape. With more and more consumers turning to their smartphones and tablets to make purchases, it is crucial for e-commerce websites to ensure that their platforms are optimized for mobile devices. This not only improves the user experience but also plays a significant role in improving search engine rankings.

One of the key aspects of mobile optimization for e-commerce sites is responsive design. This means that the website is able to adapt to different screen sizes and resolutions, ensuring that the user experience remains consistent across all devices. A responsive design not only improves user experience but also helps in boosting SEO rankings as Google prioritizes mobile-friendly websites in its search results.

In addition to responsive design, e-commerce websites should also focus on improving site speed for mobile users. Slow loading times can lead to high bounce rates, which in turn can negatively impact search engine rankings. By optimizing images, reducing server response times, and minimizing the use of heavy scripts, e-commerce sites can improve site speed and provide a better user experience for mobile users.

Another important aspect of mobile optimization for e-commerce sites is ensuring that the checkout process is streamlined and easy to use on mobile devices. Mobile users are often looking for quick and convenient ways to make purchases, so it is crucial for e-commerce websites to simplify the checkout process and eliminate any unnecessary steps. This not only improves conversion rates but also enhances the overall user experience.

Overall, mobile optimization for e-commerce sites plays a crucial role in improving search engine rankings, user experience, and conversion rates. By focusing on responsive design, site speed, and streamlined checkout processes, e-commerce websites can ensure that they are providing the best possible experience for mobile users. In today's competitive online marketplace, mobile optimization is no longer optional but essential for success.

Chapter 6: Technical SEO Audit and Analysis

Website speed optimization

In the competitive world of online marketing, website speed optimization is crucial for success. A slow-loading website can frustrate users and lead to high bounce rates, which can negatively impact your search engine rankings. In this subchapter, we will explore the importance of website speed optimization and provide you with practical tips to improve the performance of your website.

One of the main reasons why website speed optimization is essential for SEO success is because Google considers page speed as a ranking factor. In other words, faster websites are more likely to rank higher in search engine results pages (SERPs) than slower websites. This means that if you want to improve your Google rankings and increase organic traffic to your website, you need to prioritize website speed optimization.

There are several factors that can affect the speed of your website, including server performance, image size, and the use of unnecessary plugins and scripts. To optimize your website speed, start by conducting a technical SEO audit and analysis to identify areas that need improvement. This will help you pinpoint specific issues that are slowing down your website and come up with a plan to address them.

In addition to technical SEO audit and analysis, there are several on-page SEO best practices that you can implement to improve the speed of your website. For example, optimizing images by reducing their size and using appropriate file formats can significantly reduce loading times. You can also minify CSS and JavaScript files, leverage browser caching, and enable compression to further enhance your website's performance.

Off-page SEO tactics can also play a role in website speed optimization. For example, if you have a high number of external links pointing to your website, this can slow down your website's loading speed. By monitoring and managing your backlink profile, you can ensure that your website remains fast and efficient. Overall, by prioritizing website speed optimization, you can improve user experience, boost your search engine rankings, and ultimately drive more traffic and conversions to your website.

Mobile responsiveness

In today's digital age, having a website that is mobile responsive is crucial for success in the online world. With the majority of internet users now accessing websites on their mobile devices, it is more important than ever to ensure that your site is optimized for mobile viewing. This subchapter will delve into the importance of mobile responsiveness and provide tips and strategies for ensuring that your website is mobile-friendly.

One of the key benefits of having a mobile-responsive website is improved user experience. When a website is not optimized for mobile viewing, users may have difficulty navigating the site, reading content, or completing actions such as making a purchase. This can lead to frustration and ultimately result in users leaving your site and potentially turning to a competitor. By ensuring that your website is mobile responsive, you can provide a seamless and enjoyable experience for users on all devices.

Another important reason to prioritize mobile responsiveness is for search engine optimization (SEO) purposes. Google and other search engines have placed a strong emphasis on mobile-friendliness as a ranking factor. Websites that are not optimized for mobile viewing may be penalized in search engine rankings, making it harder for potential customers to find your site. By ensuring that your website is mobile responsive, you can improve your chances of ranking higher in search engine results and attracting more organic traffic.

When it comes to e-commerce SEO strategies, mobile responsiveness is especially important. With the rise of mobile shopping, it is essential for e-commerce websites to provide a seamless shopping experience on all devices. By optimizing your site for mobile viewing, you can increase conversions and drive more sales. Additionally, having a mobile-responsive website can help to build trust with customers and improve brand loyalty.

In conclusion, mobile responsiveness is a critical aspect of any SEO strategy. By ensuring that your website is optimized for mobile viewing, you can improve user experience, boost search engine rankings, and drive more traffic and conversions. Whether you are a small business owner or a large e-commerce retailer, prioritizing mobile responsiveness is key to success in the competitive online landscape.

Structured data markup

Structured data markup is a crucial component of any successful SEO strategy. In simple terms, structured data markup is a way of organizing and labeling website content in a way that search engines can easily understand. By utilizing structured data markup, website owners can help search engines better index and display their content in search results, ultimately improving their visibility and click-through rates.

One of the most popular forms of structured data markup is Schema.org, a collaborative effort by major search engines like Google, Bing, Yahoo, and Yandex to create a universal vocabulary for structured data. By adding Schema.org markup to your website, you can provide search engines with valuable information about your content, such as product prices, reviews, ratings, and event details, which can greatly enhance your search engine listings.

Implementing structured data markup is not only beneficial for search engines, but also for users. By providing search engines with more context about your content, you can help them deliver more relevant and informative search results to users. This can lead to higher click-through rates, increased traffic, and ultimately, more conversions for your website.

To implement structured data markup on your website, you can use various tools and plugins that generate the necessary code for you. Additionally, Google offers a Structured Data Markup Helper tool that can guide you through the process of adding structured data to your website. Remember to test your markup using Google's Structured Data Testing Tool to ensure that it is correctly implemented and error-free.

In conclusion, structured data markup is a powerful SEO tool that can help improve your website's visibility, click-through rates, and overall user experience. By incorporating structured data markup into your SEO strategy, you can enhance your website's search engine listings and provide users with more relevant and engaging search results. Don't overlook the importance of structured data markup in your SEO efforts – it could be the key to unlocking your website's full potential in the competitive online landscape.

Chapter 7: Top Google Ranking Techniques

Google algorithm updates

Google algorithm updates are crucial to understand for anyone working in the field of Search Engine Optimization (SEO). These updates can have a significant impact on a website's search rankings and visibility. Keeping up to date with the latest algorithm changes is essential for maintaining and improving a website's performance in search results.

One of the most well-known Google algorithm updates is the Penguin update, which targeted websites with spammy backlink profiles. This update penalized websites that engaged in black hat SEO tactics such as buying links or participating in link schemes. By understanding the implications of the Penguin update, SEO professionals can ensure that their websites comply with Google's guidelines and avoid penalties.

Another important Google algorithm update is the Panda update, which focuses on content quality and user experience. Websites with thin, low-quality content were hit hard by this update, while websites with high-quality, valuable content saw a boost in search rankings. By prioritizing content quality and user experience, websites can improve their chances of ranking well in Google's search results.

The Fred update is another Google algorithm update that targeted websites with low-quality content and aggressive advertising tactics. Websites that were overly focused on monetization at the expense of user experience were penalized by this update. By creating high-quality, user-focused content and avoiding aggressive advertising tactics, websites can ensure that they remain in Google's good graces and maintain their search rankings.

In conclusion, staying informed about Google algorithm updates is essential for anyone working in the field of SEO. By understanding the implications of algorithm changes such as Penguin, Panda, and Fred, SEO professionals can adjust their strategies to comply with Google's guidelines and improve their websites' performance in search results. By prioritizing content quality, user experience, and ethical SEO practices, websites can ensure long-term success in the ever-changing landscape of search engine optimization.

Local SEO strategies

Local SEO strategies are crucial for businesses looking to attract customers in their specific geographical area. In order to optimize for local search, businesses must focus on a variety of tactics that will help them rank higher in local search results. One important strategy is to ensure that your business is listed on Google My Business and other local directories. By claiming and optimizing your business listing, you can ensure that potential customers can easily find your business when searching for local services or products.

Another key aspect of local SEO is to focus on creating high-quality, localized content. This means creating content that is specifically tailored to your target audience in your local area. By incorporating local keywords and phrases into your content, you can increase your chances of ranking higher in local search results. Additionally, creating content that is relevant and useful to your local audience can help establish your business as a trusted authority in your niche.

In addition to creating localized content, businesses should also focus on building high-quality backlinks from other local businesses and websites. By getting backlinks from reputable local sources, you can increase your website's authority and credibility in the eyes of search engines. This can help improve your rankings in local search results and drive more traffic to your website.

Furthermore, businesses should also focus on optimizing their website for mobile users. With more and more people using mobile devices to search for local businesses, it's essential that your website is mobile-friendly and easy to navigate on smaller screens. By ensuring that your website is optimized for mobile users, you can improve your chances of ranking higher in local search results and attracting more local customers.

Overall, local SEO is a critical component of any business's digital marketing strategy. By implementing the right tactics, such as optimizing your Google My Business listing, creating localized content, building high-quality backlinks, and optimizing your website for mobile users, you can improve your chances of ranking higher in local search results and attracting more customers in your local area.

Featured snippets and rich snippets

Featured snippets and rich snippets are two important concepts in the world of search engine optimization (SEO). Featured snippets are the selected search results that are displayed at the top of the search engine results page (SERP) in a box. These snippets provide users with a concise answer to their search query, making it easier for them to find the information they are looking for quickly. Rich snippets, on the other hand, are enhanced search results that include additional information such as ratings, reviews, and images. These snippets help to make your website stand out in the search results and can increase the likelihood of users clicking on your site.

One of the main benefits of featured snippets and rich snippets is that they can help to improve your website's visibility in the search results. By optimizing your content to appear in these snippets, you can increase the chances of your website being seen by potential customers. This can lead to an increase in organic traffic and ultimately, more conversions and sales for your business. Additionally, featured snippets and rich snippets can help to establish your website as a trusted source of information in your industry, which can further enhance your online reputation.

In order to optimize your content for featured snippets and rich snippets, there are a few key strategies to keep in mind. First, you should focus on providing clear and concise answers to common search queries related to your industry. This will increase the chances of your content being selected for a featured snippet. Additionally, you should use structured data markup on your website to help search engines understand the content on your site and display rich snippets in the search results. By following these strategies, you can improve your chances of appearing in featured snippets and rich snippets and drive more traffic to your website.

When it comes to e-commerce SEO strategies, featured snippets and rich snippets can play a crucial role in helping you to stand out from your competitors. By optimizing your product pages to appear in these snippets, you can increase the visibility of your products in the search results and attract more customers to your site. For example, you can use schema markup to display product ratings and reviews in the search results, which can help to build trust with potential customers and increase the likelihood of them making a purchase. By incorporating featured snippets and rich snippets into your e-commerce SEO strategy, you can drive more organic traffic to your site and boost your sales.

In conclusion, featured snippets and rich snippets are powerful tools that can help to improve your website's visibility in the search results and attract more traffic to your site. By optimizing your content for these snippets and using structured data markup on your website, you can increase the chances of your content being selected for a featured snippet and enhance the appearance of your search results with rich snippets. Whether you are looking to improve your Google rankings, increase conversions on your e-commerce site, or enhance your overall SEO strategy, featured snippets and rich snippets are essential components to consider. By incorporating these strategies into your SEO efforts, you can achieve greater success and stand out in the competitive online landscape.

Chapter 8: Advanced SEO Strategies For Google, Yahoo and Bing

Secret SEO Tools

In the world of search engine optimization (SEO), having the right tools at your disposal can make all the difference in achieving success. This subchapter will explore some of the best-kept secrets in the realm of SEO tools that can help take your website to the next level. From keyword research to competitor analysis, these tools will give you the edge you need to outperform the competition and climb to the top of Google rankings.

One of the most powerful tools in any SEO arsenal is SEMrush. This all-in-one SEO platform offers a wide range of features, including keyword research, site audits, backlink analysis, and more. With SEMrush, you can uncover valuable insights into your site's performance and identify opportunities for improvement. Whether you're a beginner or an expert in SEO, SEMrush is a must-have tool for any digital marketer looking to boost their online visibility.

Another essential tool for any SEO professional is Ahrefs. This comprehensive SEO tool offers a range of features, including keyword research, competitor analysis, and backlink tracking. With Ahrefs, you can uncover valuable insights into your competitors' strategies and identify opportunities to improve your own website's performance. By utilizing Ahrefs, you can stay one step ahead of the competition and drive more organic traffic to your site.

For those looking to improve their on-page SEO, Moz Pro is a valuable tool to have in your arsenal. This SEO platform offers a range of features, including site audits, keyword research, and rank tracking. With Moz Pro, you can identify technical issues that may be holding your site back and optimize your content for maximum visibility in search engines. By utilizing Moz Pro, you can ensure that your website is following best practices for on-page SEO and improve your chances of ranking higher in Google search results.

In addition to these tools, there are also a number of lesser-known SEO tools that can help take your website to the next level. Tools like Screaming Frog, SpyFu, and Serpstat offer unique features that can help you uncover valuable insights into your site's performance and identify opportunities for improvement. By incorporating these tools into your SEO strategy, you can stay one step ahead of the competition and achieve greater success in the world of search engine optimization.

In conclusion, having the right tools at your disposal is essential for achieving success in the world of SEO. By utilizing powerful tools like SEMrush, Ahrefs, and Moz Pro, you can uncover valuable insights into your site's performance and identify opportunities for improvement. Additionally, lesser-known tools like Screaming Frog, SpyFu, and Serpstat can offer unique features that can help take your website to the next level. By incorporating these tools into your SEO strategy, you can outperform the competition and climb to the top of Google rankings.

Yahoo SEO Tips

In this subchapter, we will discuss some valuable Yahoo SEO tips that can help you improve your search engine rankings and drive more traffic to your website. While Google may be the dominant search engine, Yahoo still has a significant share of the market, and optimizing your site for Yahoo can help you reach a wider audience.

One important Yahoo SEO tip is to focus on creating high-quality, relevant content that is optimized for the keywords your target audience is searching for. Yahoo, like Google, values content that is informative, engaging, and well-written, so make sure to create content that meets these criteria. Additionally, be sure to include your target keywords in your content in a natural and organic way to help improve your rankings on Yahoo.

Another important Yahoo SEO tip is to optimize your website for mobile devices. With more people than ever using smartphones and tablets to access the internet, it's essential that your website is mobile-friendly. Yahoo rewards websites that are optimized for mobile devices with higher rankings, so be sure to test your site on different devices and make any necessary adjustments to ensure a seamless user experience.

Additionally, focusing on local SEO can help improve your rankings on Yahoo. Yahoo places a high value on local search results, so optimizing your website for local keywords and including your business's address, phone number, and other contact information can help improve your rankings in local search results. Be sure to also claim and optimize your business's listing on Yahoo Local to further boost your local SEO efforts.

Finally, don't forget about the importance of link building for Yahoo SEO. Building high-quality, relevant backlinks to your website can help improve your rankings on Yahoo and drive more traffic to your site. Focus on building links from reputable websites in your industry and avoid any black hat SEO tactics that could harm your rankings. By following these Yahoo SEO tips, you can improve your rankings on Yahoo and drive more traffic to your website, ultimately helping you achieve your online marketing goals.

Google SEO Tips

When it comes to improving your website's ranking on Google, there are a few key tips to keep in mind. The first step is to focus on creating high-quality, relevant content that is optimized for search engines. This means using keywords strategically throughout your content, including in the title, headers, and meta descriptions.

Another important tip is to ensure that your website is mobile-friendly. Google prioritizes mobile-friendly websites in its search results, so it's crucial to make sure that your site is optimized for mobile devices. This includes using responsive design, optimizing images for mobile viewing, and ensuring that your site loads quickly on mobile devices.

In addition to creating high-quality content and optimizing your site for mobile, it's also important to focus on building backlinks to your site. Backlinks are links from other websites that point to your site, and Google considers them to be an important ranking factor. You can build backlinks by guest posting on other websites, collaborating with influencers in your industry, and creating shareable content that others will want to link to.

One often overlooked aspect of SEO is technical optimization. This includes things like optimizing your site's code, improving site speed, and fixing any broken links or errors. By conducting a technical SEO audit and analysis, you can identify areas for improvement and make changes that will help your site rank higher in Google's search results.

Overall, the key to achieving top Google rankings is to focus on creating high-quality content, optimizing your site for mobile, building backlinks, and conducting regular technical SEO audits. By following these tips and staying up-to-date on the latest SEO best practices, you can improve your site's visibility in search engine results and drive more traffic to your site.

Bing SEO Tips

In the competitive world of online advertising and search engine optimization (SEO), achieving top Google rankings is essential for success. One of the most effective ways to improve your visibility on Bing, the second largest search engine in the world, is by implementing SEO best practices tailored specifically for this platform. In this subchapter, we will explore some valuable Bing SEO tips that can help you elevate your website's rankings and drive more organic traffic.

When it comes to Bing SEO, one of the key factors to consider is the importance of high-quality content. Bing places a strong emphasis on relevancy and user experience, so creating engaging and informative content that aligns with your target audience's search intent is crucial. Make sure to conduct thorough keyword research and optimize your content with relevant keywords that are likely to be searched for on Bing.

In addition to content, another important aspect of Bing SEO is technical optimization. This includes ensuring that your website is mobile-friendly, has fast loading speeds, and is secure with HTTPS encryption. Conducting a technical SEO audit and analysis of your website can help identify any issues that may be hindering your rankings on Bing and provide insights on how to improve your site's overall performance.

On-page SEO best practices are also essential for optimizing your website for Bing. This involves optimizing your meta tags, headers, and image alt text with relevant keywords, as well as creating a clear site structure that makes it easy for Bing's crawlers to index your content. By following on-page SEO best practices, you can improve your website's visibility on Bing and increase your chances of ranking higher in search results.

Finally, off-page SEO tactics such as building high-quality backlinks and engaging with your audience on social media can also help improve your rankings on Bing. By building a strong online presence and establishing credibility within your niche, you can attract more organic traffic to your website and improve your chances of ranking higher on Bing. By implementing these Bing SEO tips, you can enhance your website's visibility, attract more organic traffic, and ultimately achieve top Google rankings in the competitive world of online advertising and search engine optimization.

Chapter 9: Monitoring and Measuring SEO Success

Google Analytics and Search Console

In the world of digital marketing, Google Analytics and Search Console are two essential tools for understanding and optimizing your website's performance. Google Analytics provides valuable insights into user behavior, traffic sources, and conversion rates, while Search Console offers data on how your site is performing in Google's search results.

Utilizing Google Analytics can help you track the effectiveness of your SEO strategies, allowing you to see which keywords are driving the most traffic to your site, which pages are performing well, and where visitors are dropping off. By analyzing this data, you can make informed decisions about where to focus your efforts for maximum impact.

Search Console, on the other hand, provides valuable information about how your site is being indexed and ranked by Google. By monitoring your site's performance in Search Console, you can identify any issues that may be affecting your rankings and take steps to address them. This can include fixing technical errors, improving site speed, and optimizing your content for search engines.

When used together, Google Analytics and Search Console can provide a comprehensive view of your website's performance and help you identify opportunities for improvement. By regularly monitoring and analyzing data from these tools, you can make data-driven decisions to improve your SEO strategies and drive more traffic to your site.

In the competitive world of SEO, having a solid understanding of Google Analytics and Search Console is essential for success. By mastering these tools and using them to inform your SEO strategies, you can improve your website's visibility in search results, drive more organic traffic, and ultimately achieve higher rankings on Google.

Key performance indicators for SEO

Key performance indicators (KPIs) are essential for measuring the success of your SEO efforts. By tracking and analyzing these metrics, you can gain valuable insights into the effectiveness of your strategies and make informed decisions to improve your search engine rankings.

One key KPI for SEO is organic traffic. This metric measures the number of visitors coming to your website from search engines like Google, Bing, and Yahoo. By monitoring your organic traffic over time, you can see if your SEO efforts are driving more visitors to your site and ultimately increasing your visibility online.

Another important KPI for SEO is keyword rankings. This metric tracks where your website ranks in search engine results pages (SERPs) for specific keywords related to your business. By monitoring your keyword rankings, you can identify opportunities to improve your content and optimize your website for better performance in search results.

Conversion rate is another crucial KPI for SEO. This metric measures the percentage of visitors who take a desired action on your website, such as making a purchase, signing up for a newsletter, or filling out a contact form. By tracking your conversion rate, you can determine the effectiveness of your SEO strategies in driving valuable leads and sales for your business.

Finally, backlink profile is a key KPI for SEO. Backlinks are links from other websites that point to your site, and they are an important factor in determining your website's authority and credibility in the eyes of search engines. By monitoring your backlink profile, you can assess the quality and quantity of backlinks pointing to your site and identify opportunities to build more high-quality links to improve your SEO performance.

In conclusion, tracking key performance indicators for SEO is essential for evaluating the success of your strategies and making data-driven decisions to improve your search engine rankings. By monitoring metrics like organic traffic, keyword rankings, conversion rate, and backlink profile, you can gain valuable insights into the effectiveness of your SEO efforts and optimize your website for better visibility and success online.

Reporting and analysis

Reporting and analysis are essential components of any successful SEO strategy. These processes allow you to measure the effectiveness of your efforts and make data-driven decisions to improve your search engine rankings. In this subchapter, we will explore the key aspects of reporting and analysis in the context of SEO.

One of the first steps in reporting and analysis is setting up key performance indicators (KPIs) to track the success of your SEO efforts. These KPIs can include metrics such as organic traffic, keyword rankings, conversion rates, and bounce rates. By monitoring these KPIs regularly, you can identify trends and make adjustments to your strategy as needed.

In addition to tracking KPIs, it is important to conduct regular audits of your website to identify areas for improvement. This can include a technical SEO audit to identify issues such as broken links, slow page load times, and mobile usability issues. By addressing these issues, you can improve the overall user experience and increase your chances of ranking higher in search engine results.

On-page SEO best practices are also crucial for improving your search engine rankings. This includes optimizing your website's content, meta tags, and internal linking structure to make it more appealing to search engines. By following these best practices, you can increase your chances of ranking higher for your target keywords.

Finally, off-page SEO tactics such as link building and social media marketing can also play a key role in improving your search engine rankings. By building high-quality backlinks from reputable websites and engaging with your audience on social media, you can increase your website's authority and credibility in the eyes of search engines.

In conclusion, reporting and analysis are essential components of a successful SEO strategy. By setting up KPIs, conducting regular audits, following on-page SEO best practices, and implementing off-page SEO tactics, you can improve your search engine rankings and drive more organic traffic to your website. By continuously monitoring and adjusting your strategy based on data-driven insights, you can achieve SEO success and stay ahead of the competition.

Chapter 10: Conclusion and Next Steps

Recap of SEO strategies

In this subchapter, we will be providing a recap of the key SEO strategies discussed throughout this book. These strategies are essential for anyone looking to improve their website's visibility and ranking on search engines like Google. Whether you are new to SEO or looking to enhance your current tactics, these strategies will help you achieve success in the competitive online landscape.

One of the most important SEO strategies we discussed is the importance of keyword research. By identifying the most relevant and high-volume keywords for your website, you can optimize your content to attract more organic traffic. Keyword research is the foundation of any successful SEO campaign and should be regularly updated to reflect changes in search trends and user behavior.

Another crucial SEO strategy is optimizing your website's on-page elements. This includes optimizing your meta tags, headings, and content to ensure that search engines can easily crawl and index your site. By incorporating relevant keywords into your content and meta tags, you can improve your chances of ranking higher in search engine results pages (SERPs).

Off-page SEO tactics are also essential for improving your website's visibility and ranking. This involves building high-quality backlinks from reputable websites, as well as engaging with your audience on social media platforms. By creating a strong online presence and building relationships with other websites, you can improve your website's authority and credibility in the eyes of search engines.

Technical SEO audit and analysis are also critical for ensuring that your website is optimized for search engines. By regularly auditing your website's technical elements, such as site speed, mobile-friendliness, and security, you can identify and fix any issues that may be hindering your SEO performance. This will help improve your website's user experience and overall search engine ranking.

In conclusion, by implementing these SEO strategies, you can improve your website's visibility and ranking on search engines like Google. Whether you are a beginner or an experienced SEO professional, these strategies are essential for achieving success in the competitive online landscape. By focusing on keyword research, on-page optimization, off-page tactics, and technical audit, you can enhance your website's performance and attract more organic traffic.

Continuing education and staying updated

Continuing education and staying updated are crucial aspects of success in the ever-evolving world of SEO. As algorithms change and new technologies emerge, it is important for professionals in the advertising and search engine optimization industries to stay current on the latest trends and best practices. By continuously learning and adapting to the latest developments in SEO, professionals can ensure that they are providing the most effective strategies for their clients and staying ahead of the competition.

One of the best ways to stay updated on the latest trends in SEO is to attend industry conferences and workshops. These events provide a valuable opportunity to hear from experts in the field, network with other professionals, and gain insights into the latest strategies and techniques. By attending these events, professionals can stay informed about the latest changes in search engine algorithms, learn about new tools and technologies, and gain valuable insights into emerging trends in the industry.

In addition to attending conferences and workshops, professionals in the SEO industry can also benefit from ongoing training and certification programs. By obtaining certifications in areas such as Google Rankings, E-commerce SEO strategies, and Technical SEO audit and analysis, professionals can demonstrate their expertise and credibility to clients and employers. These certifications can also help professionals stay updated on the latest best practices and techniques in the field, ensuring that they are providing the most effective strategies for their clients.

Another important aspect of staying updated in the SEO industry is to regularly read industry blogs, newsletters, and publications. By following leading industry experts and staying informed about the latest news and trends, professionals can ensure that they are up-to-date on the latest developments in the field. This information can help professionals identify new opportunities, stay ahead of the competition, and provide the most effective strategies for their clients.

In conclusion, continuing education and staying updated are essential for success in the fast-paced world of SEO. By attending industry events, obtaining certifications, and regularly reading industry publications, professionals can ensure that they are providing the most effective strategies for their clients and staying ahead of the competition. By staying informed about the latest trends and best practices in the field, professionals can position themselves as experts in SEO and provide valuable insights and strategies for their clients.

Taking your SEO skills to the next level

In this subchapter, we will explore how you can take your SEO skills to the next level and become an expert in the field of search engine optimization. As an advertising or SEO professional, it is crucial to stay ahead of the game and constantly improve your knowledge and skills to achieve top Google rankings for your clients. By mastering advanced SEO strategies and tactics, you can position yourself as a valuable asset in the ever-evolving world of digital marketing.

One key aspect of taking your SEO skills to the next level is understanding the importance of E-commerce SEO strategies. For businesses that operate online, optimizing their websites for search engines is essential for driving traffic and increasing sales. By implementing effective E-commerce SEO strategies such as keyword research, content optimization, and technical SEO improvements, you can help your clients achieve higher visibility and attract more potential customers to their online stores.

Another crucial step in advancing your SEO skills is mastering technical SEO audit and analysis. Technical SEO plays a vital role in optimizing websites for search engines by addressing issues such as site speed, mobile-friendliness, and crawlability. By conducting thorough technical SEO audits and analysis, you can identify and fix any underlying issues that may be hindering your clients' websites from ranking higher on Google.

Furthermore, mastering on-page SEO best practices is essential for improving the visibility and relevance of your clients' websites in search engine results. By optimizing elements such as meta tags, headings, and content structure, you can create a more user-friendly and search engine-friendly website that ranks higher in Google. Additionally, implementing schema markup and rich snippets can help enhance your clients' search engine listings and attract more clicks from potential customers.

Lastly, off-page SEO tactics such as link building and social media marketing play a crucial role in boosting your clients' website authority and credibility in the eyes of search engines. By developing a strong backlink profile and engaging with your target audience on social media platforms, you can improve your clients' online visibility and drive more organic traffic to their websites. By mastering these advanced SEO strategies and tactics, you can take your SEO skills to the next level and achieve top Google rankings for your clients, solidifying your reputation as an expert in the field of search engine optimization.

www.ingramcontent.com/pod-product-compliance
Lightning Source LLC
Chambersburg PA
CBHW070950220526
45471CB00007B/2965